THE SHADOWS FALL BEHIND

The Shadows Fall Behind

Poems by

Margo Button

OOLICHAN BOOKS
LANTZVILLE, BRITISH COLUMBIA, CANADA
2000

Copyright © 2000 by Margo Button. ALL RIGHTS RESERVED. No part of this publication may be reproduced, stored in a retrieval system, or transmitted, in any form or by any means, without prior written permission of the publisher, except by a reviewer who may quote brief passages in a review to be printed in a newspaper or magazine or broadcast on radio or television; or, in the case of photocopying or other reprographic copying, a licence from CANCOPY (Canadian Copyright Licensing Agency), 6 Adelaide Street East, Suite 900, Toronto, Ontario M5C 1H6.

Canadian Cataloguing in Publication Data

Button, Margo, 1938-
   The shadows fall behind

ISBN 0-88982-184-4

   I. Title.
PS8553.U873S52   2000   C811'.54   C00-910359-7
PR9199.3.B88S52 2000

We gratefully acknowledge the support of the Canada Council for the Arts for our publishing program.

THE CANADA COUNCIL | LE CONSEIL DES ARTS
FOR THE ARTS | DU CANADA
SINCE 1957 | DEPUIS 1957

Grateful acknowledgement is also made to the BC Ministry of Tourism, Small Business and Culture for their financial support.

We acknowledge the financial support of the Government of Canada through the Book Publishing Industry Development Program for our publishing activities.   Canadä

Cover image by Eva Wynand

Published by
Oolichan Books
P.O. Box 10, Lantzville
British Columbia, Canada
V0R 2H0

Printed in Canada by
Morriss Printing Company,
Victoria

For Ron and Andrea

Acknowledgements

Some of the poems in this collection were published in *Fiddlehead, The Antigonish Review, Contemporary Voices 2, West Word, Event, Dandelion, Prairie Fire, This Magazine* and *Room of One's Own*. Poems have appeared in the 1995-96 *Anthology of Magazine Verse* and *Yearbook of American Poetry; Sandburg-Livesay Anthology*, 1998 and 1999 and *Vintage* 1994, 1996 and 1998. "New Messiah" was short-listed for the 1997 Berkshire Prize and "Easter Sunday" placed third in the 1998 Petra Kenney Prize.

I wish to thank:

Elizabeth MacDonell (*If I Played My Life*), Anne Michaels (*Fugitive Pieces*) and Nancy Wood (*Spirit Walker*) whose books provided useful source material.

The Island Writers of Nanaimo for their eagle eyes and our magical journey together: Win Baker, Linda Martin, Kit Pepper, K. Louise Schmidt, Leanne Smith, Millie Tremblay, Ursula Vaira, Joan Van Der Goes, Alison Watt and Sue Wheeler, all of whom have given me incisive suggestions over the past three years while this book was in progress.

Patricia Young, Leanne Smith, Ron Smith and Ursula Vaira for being such fine editors and a pleasure to work with.

My niece, Natasha Thorpe whose Arctic adventures became my son's in "The Dead Have Birthdays".

Eva Wynand whose painting conveys the spirit of my book.

My husband Ron for his love and support and my daughter, Andrea, who keeps me smiling.

Contents

The Colour of a Ghost

- 15 Easter Sunday
- 16 Pietà
- 17 What is the Colour of a Ghost?
- 18 Uprooted
- 19 Checkmate
- 21 Refugees
- 22 Bones and the Blue
- 24 The Gazebo – A Circle That Always Leads Home
- 25 Treasure
- 27 First Love
- 28 A Piece of Him I Puzzled Over
- 29 Though You Are Dead I Hang on to You
- 30 Replicas
- 31 Out of the Blue
- 32 When I was a Girl
  Tragedy was Someone Else's Story
- 33 Necessary Distances

34 The Fish
35 The Butterfly Effect
36 Canyon de Chelly
37 Spirit-Keepers
38 The Loved One Speaks
39 Tuktu, The Wanderer
40 The Dead Have Birthdays

Blood of the Sun, Seeds of the Sun

47 Puerto Vallarta
48 Villa Media Luna
49 Hibiscus
50 Chenille
51 The Caracole Vine
52 Pregnant Women with Complications
53 Diego and Frida Rivera, 1931
54 Day of the Dead
56 Blood of the Sun, Seeds of the Sun

We Come from a Good Family

61 We Come from a Good Family
62 The Wool-Winder
64 Glory-Hole 1
65 Glory-Hole 2
66 The Lie
68 He Made Her Pregnant
70 The Sideshow
71 Close as Wax
72 Well, Sir
73 I Can Still Say Hello and Good-bye
74 Such Goings-On
75 Scheherazade

A Wealth of Extra Parts

- 81 The Theatre
- 83 Umbra Nihili
- 84 The Ocean and Wilderness I Am
- 85 Flustration
- 86 A Certain Age
- 88 Motorcycle Accident
- 89 To Be
- 91 Bad Girl
- 92 Gossip
- 93 The Corset-Maker
- 94 Stigmata
- 95 jenni+pooh.bear.com
- 96 The Slave – Fantasy by an Unknown Artist
- 97 The New Messiah
- 98 L'Acte Gratuit
- 99 Forgive us Our Trespasses
- 100 On a Bus to the Everglades
- 102 Alfred Hitchcock Dolls
- 103 Touchstones
- 105 Andrea de Los Angeles

The Colour of a Ghost

For Randall, 1967-1994

*Missing me one place, search another,
I stop somewhere waiting for you.*
— Walt Whitman

Easter Sunday

                  The guests have gone.
I make turkey soup, chop onions, celery, carrots,
add them to the carcass.

                  The radio is company:
*In Sicily, on Good Friday, women wear black
to lament the crucifixion.*

                  Three years since my son died,
his ashes dispersed in the swoofing grey sea. I watch
from the kitchen as it swallows, swells, swallows again.

                  Last night, as logs sloughed
on shore, I woke in dread, wanting to search the beach
for bits of bone.

                  The broth boils over, hisses
a homey aroma. I like making soup, something out of
nothing but leftovers. An anchor on the hearth.

                  To warm the cockles.
My heart breaks at Easter. Brutal death,
grieving mother. I should have worn black
instead of the rage I could not explain.

Pietà

I know the massive weight she bears, marble
body sprawled across her legs, upbearing
the man-child she lived to protect.
Huge with grief, she tries to
encompass his gangliness
while he subsides, long limbs
reaching away from her
down into the earth. No blood stains
the white folds of her skirt, yet she bleeds.
If only she had not colluded
with the flattering angel, allowed
Jehovah to have his way.
What does she care for glory?
She eases him into the grave, longing
to follow where she should have led.

What is the Colour of a Ghost?

I put on your old jacket, search the pockets
as I stroll around the garden. You are not
there on the mossy bench by the sea.
A pair of geese swoops down over the house
honking loud enough to wake the dead

but you do not hear. Red tulip petals
scatter across the lawn. I lead you to
clouds of pink clematis, but you
could care less about the resurrection of spring.
All day I wait for the phone to ring, your soft voice.

The third anniversary of your death, nobody calls.
Everyone is out shopping or planting annuals.
I pull the blinds and crawl into bed, remember
how, as a child, you made houses of chairs and quilts,
sat for hours inside the dark.

Uprooted

   Thrust up on our beach in a storm
      The stump has no recall of pulsing sap
         Or giant arms riding the winds
            Eagles in the crown   Starlings in the heart

Its weathered grey roots   A ganglia
      Of severed nerves   Like his brain
         An arbour afloat

The family tree   Truncated
      When the last male died   My son
         Stood here one day at seventeen

Surveying our house and land   Declared
     Someday this will all be mine
        As if he would always be
           Standing here by the cellophane sea

Checkmate

You needn't have died.

> *I had to die.*

You died a long time ago. Far away.

> *Nearby. Out of sight. Out of mind.*

Never off my mind.

> *I asked for a new brain
> for my birthday.*

If I hadn't gone out that evening
while you stayed home alone.

> *The devil left a message
> on the answering machine.*

If I hadn't brought you home for the week-end.
If I'd said you could live here. There.

> *He wanted to see me.*

If I hadn't insisted you go back to hospital.

> *Shut the windows, turn off the tv -
> jibber-jabbering voices
> blame me.*

If I hadn't left knives in the kitchen.

                        Scissors in the drawer.
                        Sleeping pills in the cabinet.

If I'd checked your room when I came home.
If I hadn't gone to bed and slept soundly.

                        The body on the steps
                        might have been you.

I should have known.

                        You did know.

Refugees

Every heart to love will come but like a refugee.
                                                    – Rumi

A woman thanks me
for putting words in her mouth
as if my poems are a refuge after the flood,
an ark to shelter in
till she arrives on dry ground.
I told my story, she tells hers –
a covenant we understand.

My daughter was an only child.
She wanted to be a scientist.

I've never met this woman
but I know she has a hole in her heart
and no child to crawl back in.
She envies her friends
when their children get married
and she doesn't want to hear about
grandchildren who are
spitting images. Television news
burns her eyes;
love takes her by surprise

for the college girls raped in Guatemala,
shining hair dragged through mud;
for the Oklahoma mothers
whose children blew up.
Love for the bomber Kaczynski,
his brother who betrayed him,
for their mother who could not provide
a haven for her child.

Bones and the Blue

*My pleasant disposition likes the world with
nobody in it.*
                        – Georgia O'Keeffe

At Ghost Ranch she caressed
a bleached vertebrae
as if it were a lover's spine.
Her black habit revealed nothing
but a triangle of weathered face and neck,
the same shape as the skull
grinning behind her on the wall.

She gathered cowbones instead of friends,
dragged them back to paint in her studio,
teasing us with *trompe l'oeil* –
through a cow's pelvis, a blue egg of sky.

> There is another painting – not hers –
> of a broken eggshell
> given me by a friend
> when my son took his life.

O'Keeffe removed every cloud that cluttered the
sky,
pulled desert clean out of its shadows.
Did she mourn her child
unborn, her child's children?

My image – more indelible than paint –
is of him sprawled on the steps,
gazing at clouds –
the melting and settling
of my bones into the ground
as I eavesdropped on his death
and the sun went on shining.

The Gazebo –
A Circle That Always Leads Home

From the cliff I gaze back at seals,
an orca in jester's costume.
Mink scuttle across the rocks,
save their skreeking for moonlit nights.
They disappear, the sea resurrects them.

On the beach are drifting graves of wood,
bleached trunks tossed up in winter,
knots exposed, rusty hearts
alive with wood beetles. One log is pierced
by a long spike and chain.

After you died we built a spirit house
for you – a gazebo,
the foundation of river stones
you'd gathered one day with your father.

Come, slip under the arches –
they face every wind – a circle
that always leads home. Rest a while
in the still hot air. There's a cedar chair,
a book and pen, the dog's bone.

Treasure

For where your treasure is, there will your heart also be.
                        – Matthew 6:19

A bloodstone horse from China
canters across the marble mantel.
I want to grab the streaming mane, gallop
back to years when our son was alive.

In Nepal we climbed through
forests of rhododendron,
watched clouds scroll, unscroll
the holy peaks of the Himalayas.

He smoked a hubble-bubble in Kathmandu.
Our daughter walked around
a Buddhist shrine – huge eyes on its walls
like those of babies outlined in kohl.

Kashmir in cherry blossom time,
the four of us rocked to sleep
in a houseboat across from Shalimar.
We trekked the hills on horseback,
washed our hair in a glacial spring.
In Srinagar he bartered his jacket for
a jewelled dagger he gave you,
a coarse woolen shawl for me.

We brought home silk rugs
strewn with flowers, chants of fathers and sons
who weave in dark rooms.
And Tibetan prayer wheels –
trinkets to amuse the deaf gods.

First Love

In the photo your heads are together;
your arm never leaves her side.
She still wears the little-girl dress
she wore at your graduation.
You're in a new striped suit –
the one we buried you in.

She wrote today, the first time since
you died, said she had a lot of feelings
but didn't specify. She still calls me *Mrs.*,
said it's her upbringing,
the same shy girl who dared to date a *gweilo*
when her parents disapproved.

At seventeen, you were a colourful cock rooster,
legs too long for your britches.
You sneaked the family car to drive her
around Hong Kong island. Took her sailing,
donned a woolen cap to show her
the Sundance Kid. You taught her
how a *foreign devil* loves.

You introduced her to her own town –
a restaurant in the back streets
where a waiter grabbed a snake,
smashed it on the sidewalk until it went limp.
Those were silly times, she said in her letter:
the two of you sitting on rickety chairs,
sipping the steaming soup,
snakes slithering in cages along the wall.

27

A Piece of Him I Puzzled Over

in that ransacked apartment
on the bathroom door he pasted
a ragged page torn from Vogue

two young women cloaked
head to toe in funereal black
blurred as they careen down the street
one on roller blades
                leans
on her friend running in high heels
both on the verge of
                falling off-
kilter   drunk on high fashion
one long leg revealed
in see-through chiffon
hardly a pin-up
to turn a young man on

today I discovered
a stain on the woman's groin
where the pebbled page had been wet
where he'd pressed himself
against the door

Though You Are Dead I Hang on to You

Like the old servant in Savannah
dressed in bowler hat and Sunday suit
who takes an invisible dog for a walk.

Rigid leash and collar stretch out before him,
a divining rod to the underworld.
Every day he tips his hat at passers-by

who play along with the dog
that never chases possums
or pees on magnolias.

When asked why he walks a phantom,
he claims it was his master's last wish.
If he doesn't take the dog out, who will?

Replicas

when I go away I leave your photos home
    take the negatives with me
the house might catch fire
    your likeness go up in flames

brooding child with Amazon parrot
    teenage sailor on Spring Moon
lithe body   melting curve of neck
    kneeling youth in a Shinto temple

the undertaker's photo   your gaunt face
    rejuvenated in death
your father sister and I   one-dimensional
    speechless at your side

why be afraid   in dreams I follow you
    curly hair backlit   a dead ringer
you take my hand   lead me back
    across rubble to family who remain

Out of the Blue

Nelson, New Zealand

We rented a house for three months –
doilies and drooping African violets,
pink plush living and dining –
colours over-coordinated.

Old photos in the hall – four sepia babies
whose pale cheeks, watery eyes
do not betray who dies young.
Out of the blue, the owner said,
at thirty – her son, a big man.
His aorta was the size of a child's.

Long legs stretch across the frame
as he relaxes in the last photo, a picture of health
with wife and four children
only days before the artery exploded –
a star casting him into space.

Dark eyes bore holes
through his mother's lace curtains,
past the roses and jasmine
that hug the house, jostle for room,
reaching through slats to the other side –
a field where gaudy parachutists
drop from the sky
like short-lived blooms.

When I was a Girl
Tragedy was Someone Else's Story

I came to Grief willingly, welcomed her
like an old friend I had known in other lives.
She hides in her room and cries, Mom said.

So I wept more. Operas taught me
tragic roles. Saturdays in my bedroom
tuned to a plastic radio, I dressed in scarves,

made myself up in the mirror. At the Met
I was a prima donna with a magical name:
Renata Tebaldi. Victoria de los Angeles,

singing Eurydice in Hades, felled by the gods
when Orpheus disobeyed.
The demented Lucia: *"Oh Dire Misfortune."*

Entombed with my lover, I sang Aida
till the last breath – *"Oh to Die so Pure and Lovely!"*
Then I gathered roses on the stage.

Necessary Distances

for Harold Button, 1910-1998

Another autumn between us,
   another subtracted landscape.
      Broad maple leaves
         reach up from the ground

like old men's rusted fingers
   pushing us farther apart –
      necessary distances you taught me
         when death laid hands on you,

young man out of time.
   This week was your Grandpa's turn –
      a short easy unwinding,
         fitting for the old

gentleman who sat in the back seat
   so he could tip his hat to the ladies.
      The raconteur who forgot your name
         helped you disappear after you died.

The day of his funeral, the remaining
   grandchildren flung his ashes
      into the same waves that swallowed yours
         while their children went on playing.

The Fish

Under house arrest, we wade about in a room
up to our knees in a reeking primeval soup.
Fish float belly up. A small limp one
I cradle in my palm – my son reincarnated.

I search for traces of him – *Please, dear God,
any sign.* Then beg my husband who is no
magician, *Turn him back into a boy.*

At once, a huge bottom fish is upon us
with burnished scales, brash look.
Inside the massive mouth –
a child's head, familiar blue eyes.
He pries apart the razor teeth, births himself.

The Butterfly Effect

In the painting a young man walks off a cliff
    Along a glistening tightrope toward
        The end he holds in his hands.

Master of each step, he unwinds
    A beam of light into the sky. He assumes
        The moon will reveal the astral plane

He must travel like Icarus on a besotted voyage.
    My son believed he could walk on air,
        Broke pelvis and elbow, pulverized his feet.

Is it unseemly to love him so? A dead end
    To love the dead?

Canyon de Chelly

On the cliff face, Anasazi
    shamans recorded their visions:
        hands all over the canyon, life size,

hovering there in space. Hands
    hold hands. One with six fingers.
        Fingers the shape of flames

flickering messages. I fit my hand
    into a small one, a woman's perhaps,
        and I am the one who is touched

as if by a blind stranger exploring
    my face. That hand in mine,
        calloused from tilling earth, grinding grain,

a firm hand of one who lived
    uncluttered days between earth and sky.
        Her childbirth pangs no longer echo

children's laughter as they run
    among the mottled cottonwoods.
        Long juniper tongues slip down,

lick her crumbling house, the barren walls.

Spirit-Keepers

You'd like that artisan I met
in a Californian market.
She makes spirit-keepers
from scratch – small bundles of
cloth and leather bound with twine,
dressed up in beads and feathers
she unearths
in shops all over the world.

Why are their faces blank,
their bodies amorphous?
Spirit-keepers can be
anyone you want.
They huddle in her booth –
swaddled embryos
on the brink of
gathering a soul.

If I make you a body of
ghost flowers and red rosebuds,
wrap it in your blue silk shirt...
if I place your suede pouch
around the neck, rose quartz
still beating inside . . .

if I make a spirit-keeper,
will you come?

The Loved One Speaks

I watch the clouds' shadow-play
    on roseate hills, long for the high desert.

So I climb to Mastodon Peak, sit down
    with obelisks sprawling in avalanche.

In disorder, there is a splendour
    and murmur of ancient gods

who tired of Herculean labour and
    flung boulders in tantrums across the land

splintering varnished faces as they fell.
    At night, rocks huddle together to anchor stars.

In fractures of their sandstone flanks
    stand Joshua trees with open arms.

Heart thumping, dog panting at my side,
    I listen to the oriole's song.

Tuktu, The Wanderer

A huge growth like a vision –
    a dream I had years ago of antlers,
    newly formed, fluid and soft
    like a mother's arms
    embracing me in a barren season.

Each spring the caribou sprouts
a shovel above the third eye –
left-handed one year, right the next
as if directions have meaning
when you gather up the sky.

Tender-fingered tips flutter and reach –
sweet fruit the Inuit cut off and eat. Flesh
longs for flesh, bone for bone
but cannot touch – a fontanelle
not meant to close,

    a closeness not meant to last.
    Soon velvet bleeds and hangs in shreds,

tines harden
and the sparring begins –
coursing blood, willing cows.

On the tundra after their rut,
I come upon a rack.
What is it like to lay down that brief majesty,
slough off a monument to the self
and float weightless across the tundra?

The Dead Have Birthdays

Your thirtieth birthday. I daydream
you come home for the day,
returned from a long northern voyage.
You are strong and tall again, your old self.
I told you I'd be back, you say
with the same crooked grin, warm embrace.
*Where I have been
there is no word for good-bye.*

You're a man now with a certain reticence,
the woman you love at your side –
This is the one, Mom, you whisper.
She's Inuit. I imagine
your children – black eyes, blond curls.

You will tell them bedtime stories
of ling cod you speared in Schooner Cove
as a boy – the gleaming green flesh.
Summers you fished off Cape Scott,
gutted hundreds of salmon, each silver body
coating you with its armour.
A two hundred pound halibut took
three of you to pull in. You never forgot
the astonished eyes
staring from one side of its head.

Today, you bring us Arctic char.
I've baked a chocolate cake
with thirty candles that won't blow out.
We give you a dictionary
of Inuinnaqtun – you love learning
difficult languages.
Quana, you say. *Quanapiaq.*
You have a model *qayak* for your dad,
a book for me about Iqaluit women
who carve their lives out of soapstone.

So many adventures to tell –
skidooing at night across Elu Inlet
you heard the dancing green sky speak
the crackling tongues of snow.
You passed by Inuit hunters who sit
for hours hunkered over a hole in the ice
waiting for a seal to come up for air.
Quinuituq, they call it there –
deep patience.

Blood of the Sun, Seeds of the Sun

*Turn your face to the sun
and let the shadows fall behind.*

— *Maori proverb*

Puerto Vallarta

Ants swarm across the keyboard.
I shake them into the garbage
where they'll have a better meal.

The writers meet at The Lunatics Cafe.
We talk about our analysts and
the president's brother who stashed
a hundred million in a Swiss bank.

Last week, a python slid out of the jungle
and ate the neighbour's cat.
A mini van exploded, the driver inside.
Burnt ficus leaves scatter
where he stepped through the looking-glass.

Bars flourish in this tourist town.
If you buy a margarita, the second one's free.
A restaurant offers *octopussy in its own ink*.

Today, a truckload of *policía* armed with carbines
arrive at our gate and ask to use our terrace
to spot a thief who fled into the hills.

No water in the house all week-end;
still no repairman this morning.
Mondays in Mexico, not even the hens lay eggs.

Villa Media Luna

They built the villa of bricks and steel
    and tons of cement, molded it
        until a half moon house appeared
            with more window than wall.

They painted it gleaming white
    like the light that limned the balconies
        and left fly-by-nights on the floor.
            The walls were a wrinkled embrace

that rippled in the jungle winds –
    a hot sinuous song without pause.
        Windows framed palm trees' tossing manes,
        lurid sunsets, powder of stars.

And no thing was ever shut out:
    neither sleepy moths, near-sighted bees
        nor two House finches
            who thought the villa was inside out.

Hibiscus

At daybreak, I blossom wide,
hungry for light and warmth
after the crypt of earth where
the only sign of life was
rain trickling to my roots.

Bright yellow voices bloomed
above. I saw no one.
How welcome
the unfurling
I only dreamed till now.
How brazen I am
but no one sees me spread
my lips, colour of papaya.
No one tastes
my tarty tropical style.
Even you pass me by,
ignoring my skirts
a-powder with pollen.

You complain of early deaths.
Soon, I'll lie shrivelled
on the walk – a tiny parasol
wrapped in shadow.
I measure life in hours
but no regrets.
My blowsy body calls.
Before I go,
let me lean a while
into the cobalt sky.

Chenille

French: caterpillar
from Latin: canicula: little dog

1

Long red tails dangle from the chenille plant,
so supine and furry. I expect them to protest
if I caress them, to pull away, curl up tight
like my dog's tail which I groom bouffante.

Outrageous tail, outrageous bloom. I look for
busy legs, moist innards in a caterpillar plant
but tangled flowers have no pulse,
only tiny seeds unready for release.

2

Chenille reminds me of bedspreads
when I was little – soft cotton ribs
I patted like puppies or pinched with spit
so they'd stand up straight.
I pulled them out when no one was looking.

Anything to pass the time while
I was supposed to take a nap. In bed
I created my own *Land of Counterpane:*
whitecaps at sea, a beach
swept into ridges by a storm that blew and blew
until all the make-believe blew away.

The Caracole Vine

They came in the night, hordes of ants.
    You were unsuspecting, loosely attached,
climbing a surmountable wall.
    They stripped you and left you,
a tangled barbed-wire skeleton,
    all the snail-blossoms fallen.
Your roots shuddered but held.

Courage is not about climbing summits
    or planting flags. It is a puny, plodding thing,
arid, unappetizing. It has no lofty goals.
    You meander in a dreary sequence
until one day you are surprised
    by blind tendrils unspiraling.

Pregnant Women with Complications

When you are cracked open, dance.
            – Rumi

In the Zapotec ruins of Monte Alban
    is an ancient hospital, walls lined with
        bas-reliefs – textbook cases on slabs of stone.
           "The Dancers", archaeologists called them.

How could they ignore the curlicues of
    fallopian tubes that floated inside
        like musical clefs or fretwork on a violin?
           One woman squats as if her baby might

emerge like corn from the ochre soil.
    Another waits out the centuries,
        baby's legs dangling between hers.
           Ancient doctors perform Caesarians –

stones howl, hands flutter.
    In the dusty square, the jacarandas'
        atrophied seed pods gape like
           silent castanets among the blooms.

Diego and Frida Rivera, 1931

I look at how she painted him, rooted
like the shapeless colossus of Memnon – he,
the great artist with palette and brushes,
six feet tall, three hundred pounds, ramrod straight,
his legs like columns in giant boots.

The Sphinx betrayed her with her own sister.
Toad-Frog, she called him, her prince in disguise.

I see her at his side like a splint on his leg,
a pharoah's wife who barely reaches his knees,
her own feet so dainty they seem bound,
elegant head leaning toward him, their bodies
forming the letter D – he the line, she the curve.

I shudder at how she tore out her heart,
laid it on the altar of this man.

Day of the Dead

1

This bread is round, bone-
dusted for the Day of the Dead.
In the kitchen, red ants are making
a feast of it until I spray them
into confusion at their last supper.

Sweet ant bodies remind me of
skulls in the bakery window:
blue candy sockets, spun sugar hair,
names on their foreheads –
a gift for your lover –
and bon-bon cadavers
that peep out of coffins
like children tucked into bed.

2
I need to touch the skeletons
in the shop window, feel the weight
of papier maché bodies,
trace their inky bones.

In cowboy hats they loll
together like drunken friends.
Comical heads jiggling on springs
they swagger toward me –
dry-legged, loose-jointed –
grab my arm, invite me to join the fun.
They wouldn't mean to elbow me aside,
leave me lying in the gutter.

Once in France I saw a bunker
piled high with bones like cordwood in winter –
skulls here, limbs there.
But assembled here today
are the friendly dead and I'm not afraid
to make friends with strangers.

Blood of the Sun, Seeds of the Sun

Here is no fierce migration,
no thrashing upstream,
no birth-death agony,

but a hushed
biding of multitudes
in a mountain sanctuary.
Monarchs repose
from a journey begun
five generations ago,
each butterfly
encoded with a map
back to a mythic
northern land.

Oyamel firs
droop with the weight
of paper wings
like a burden of snow,
so heavy that
branches crack and
crash to the forest floor.
If you part the bushes
you will see
bright tiger wings
sprout on dying limbs.

When amber heat
swarms through
sluggish veins
they erupt in fountains.
Drops of ochre lava,
black pumice
speckle the sky.

Listen.
You can hear
the swishing of millions.

We Come from a Good Family

We Come from a Good Family

Great Aunt never married,
called no children her own.
She baked strawberry shortcake
for my sisters and me. Sent us gifts
with five-cent cards, signed *Viola*
in soft pencil so we could use them again.
Mom said she was mean as cat pee.

Every Sunday, she sat alone in the family pew
beside the pillar – a pillar of the church
like mother and grandmother before her,
singing *This is my Father's house.*

Everyone in town knew Viola
had a lover. The whole damn town knew
it was her first cousin – the undertaker
who had a family of his own. At night
she ran off to meet him at the lake,
the white light of longing
released from her corsets.
The Ouija board knew about that.

We come from a good family, Mom said.
We come from a good . . .
We come . . .

I saw the lace curtains pulled aside
when Great Aunt and I walked by –
nosy-parkers ferreting out our business.

The Wool-Winder

for Viola MacDowell, 1897-1963

1945

Great Aunt knit and purled the war away –
six years of mittens and socks
for the boys overseas. I stretched the skeins
while she wound the wool in balls.
Needles clicked and clacked, *Pray God
they all come back, back, back...*

Salty evenings by the Bay of Fundy
we snuggled close, so close on the veranda
swing, swinging while my fingers
wove in and out of the afghan
weaving us together. Nights in the parlour,
we listened to crackling voices on BBC –
Hitler and Churchill turned down low
when I climbed upstairs to sleep in her bed.

Sirens blew. The blackouts began.
I nibbled the grosgrain off the quilts,
made my body scarce under the sheets
so the Germans wouldn't see me
when they kicked in the door.

1997

The veranda has vanished, the stone steps
I jumped from when jumping was fun.
Someone asphalted the lilacs, silenced
the clamouring perfume, uprooted
the raspberries we picked in the scratchy sun.
Someone built a garage, erased
the buttercup path to the dark shed where
ice lay dripping patterns in sawdust.

I knock at the door, make excuses to enter
where I belong. My great-grandparents
built this house a hundred years ago.
The mahogany staircase
Great Aunt descended on a stretcher.
The glory-hole gone
to make room for a kitchen.
I wander the rooms feeling like Alice –
ceilings cave in, sills touch the floor.
Her bedroom of roses where I fiddled
during afternoon naps, longing for
mouse musicians to play –
the old wind-up toy she never let me touch.

I want more than intangibles.
*Perhaps there is something that is hers
in the coal cellar. I seem to remember,*
the new owner tells me. In the dark,
she reaches up to a rough black beam,
pulls down a wool-winder –
Viola written in pencil.

Glory-Hole 1

We called it the glory-hole, the little room
behind Grandma's kitchen stove
where she stored odds and ends.
I used to sneak in and pull the blinds
but she didn't like my snooping –
It is not your affair.

I unscrewed the preserves, stuck
my finger under the wax,
licked the raspberry juice
that leaked out at the edge.

In old catalogues with broken spines
I spied ladies in lacey lingerie.
Dressed up in Grandma's
peach-coloured corset,
I danced to the scratchy Victrola:
Barney Google
with the goo goo googly eyes.

Glory-Hole 2

My friend tells me that the glory-hole
    is the urinal down by Esso

where guys thrust their penises through the wall.
    The women are like attendants in a Jiffy-Lube.

They wear sanitary uniforms and rubber gloves,
    have agile fingers and mouths.

When they get bored, they chat about the town
    they grew up in, the horror movie they saw.

They tell jokes about stiffs, laugh among themselves
    like ambulance drivers at the scene of an accident.

The Lie

I was skating on thin ice
In the field across from Grandma's
In my own figure-eight world
Age six, wrapped in scarf and mittens

In the field across from Grandma's
Blades slashed and swished
Age six, wrapped in scarf and mittens
Weeds poked above the surface

Blades slashed and swished
Out of the blue, brimming with sun
Weeds poked above the surface
When the boy sing-songed

Out of the blue, brimming with sun
The chant goes with any words
When the boy sing-songed
Your mother's been married before

The chant goes with any words
I stumbled and fell; my head snapped back
Your mother's been married before
A sick, sharp crack

I stumbled and fell; my head snapped back
A brief going-away
A sick, sharp crack
My glasses lay shattered under the snow

A brief going-away
Though my mother said he lied
My glasses lay shattered under the snow
I knew what I knew

Though my mother said he lied
In my own figure-eight world
I knew what I knew
I was skating on thin ice

He Made Her Pregnant

She sobs. She doesn't want any more.
That big head of yours, she says to me –
dents of the forceps still in my skull.
Perhaps, I'm his fault too.
When she's angry, she shouts,
*You'll see what it's like to suffer
when you have your own.*

Behind the newspaper, he is the bland voice
that chuckles at Fibber McGee and Molly
and plays the music low before going to bed at ten.
I try to imagine him
pinning her with those big raw hands,
prying her legs apart, plunging.

Once I saw him drown kittens in a bucket of water,
kittens I'd just seen born – black and slimy,
eyes milky blind. His hands shoved down,
down those little pink noses hungry for air.

At night in bed, she sucks in her breath,
You're hurting me. I freeze,
breathless at the breathing behind
the curtain strung between our rooms.

Sometimes she goes out and I strut in
the pubescent dark of my room, admiring
my lovely breasts, wishing they were
pendulous like hers with swollen dark nipples.

From the living room he hears me,
comes to the door. *What's going on in here?*
I scurry into bed. Dare him to come in.

The Sideshow

Five years old, you offered
    tiny dented buttons to your doll
while your sister's sweet slurping
    danced in your head.

Your mother was amused. You wanted
    blue-veined gourds like hers.
Later came the yearning to open
    like petals thirsting for rain.

You touched the soft mounds, origins
    marvellous as starbursts. You knew
they were miracles before they emerged.
    Till the day you overheard
your mother laugh, *She's starting to show.*

Close as Wax

I never wanted to be like her
but there she is
reborn in my wooden fingers –
anger in the bones, old women say.
She displayed them for sympathy,
veering this way that
in need of direction. I'd reach out,
she'd pull back with a grimace,
refusing my touch.

She banged them, slammed them,
disowned them like wayward children.
She tried copper bracelets,
gold injections,
melted wax on the stove.

I perform the same ritual,
dip my hand in wax, let it drip,
solidify, think of Mom, dip again.
A thick glove forms – inert fingers
in amniotic fluid, an embryo's
half-formed hand – phantom nails,
spectral fingers at sixes and sevens.

Well, Sir

> *for my father, Gordon Bartlett*

That's how he starts. *Well, Sir,* he says,
his mouth twitching at the corners
as he gears up to tell another tale.
Down-East when he was a boy
he saw four-masted schooners
sail up the St. Croix, load and unload
coal and lumber and lobster crates.

When his Grandma came to visit
she drove a horse and wagon,
took a day to cover twenty miles,
shot some partridge on the way.

Six years old, he set his first trap.
The creature vanished into a burrow.
Dad, he said, *get your .22.*
*Well, Sir, he pulled out a chipmunk
but he never made fun of me.*

*Remember the Model T's?
They couldn't make it up Waweig hill.
Sunday afternoon, we'd sit on the porch
laughing as they rolled back down again.*

*Did I tell you the one about
the bear cub we shot? The boys
heaved it in the back seat. Well, Sir,
along comes a friend looking for a ride . . .*

I Can Still Say Hello and Good-bye

In the hallway, pinched apple women
slouch in a row of wingback chairs, wait
in a room for Godot. Nurses come and go.
A man is dead to the world in a wheelchair;

his hands, bruised yellow poppies in his lap.
Spindle legs push a walker. There are shouts
as we pass, *I can still say hello and good-bye!*
Mom and Dad have telescoped their lives

into one small room facing the parking lot.
Ugly curtains hang on the windows – fireproof;
they can't be changed. Dad is dying
for an ocean view. *Don't make friends,*

he tells Mom. He doesn't plan to stay.
Two chests, two chairs is all they're allowed.
The leftovers went to the grandchildren
or the dumpster. Dad says he won't be dumped

on this dung heap with all these sick people
who'll make him sick but he's too much
the gentlemen to swear. Mom arranges
her cloisonné vases; a young woman

in swishing red porcelain skirts;
a blue bird – crystal beak in full cry.
Her closet is crammed with fancy clothes.
I'll be dressing up for dinner, she says.

Such Goings-On

>　*for Hilda Button*

I put Mom's summer clothes away in a chest
while she sits on the bed giving directions.
*I worry about your father; he forgets
who I am.* No need to lower her voice
when she confides. Dad refuses a hearing aid.

*Last week, he kidnapped me for three days,
took me to a cabin down by the lake.
Yes, he did. And I lost my clothes.
How do I get them back?*

She says Lebanese men in white gloves
have taken over the dining room,
occupied all the seats. And the nurses
make a terrible racket wheeling coffins
up and down the halls at night.

I repeat her stories to Dad, ask what he thinks.
Well, he reflects,
you can't be too careful, can you?

Scheherazade

The only trips she takes are round
and round the garden at Long Term Care
slumped to the side in a wheelchair
scuff-scuffing her slippers while Dad
sits in the room, too proud for a ride.
We pass the snapdragons
whose coral throats are shut,
the mini golf green
where no one ever putts.

> *I saw them cremate a girl here,*
> *scatter her ashes on the grass.*

She tells a thousand and one tales
yet no jinni appears to do her bidding.
She slips down the road on her own,
discovers *a cosy home, a lovely couple*
with two boys and a girl
who invite her to sleep over. Each day
she embellishes. A noisy crowd of children
board upstairs. A prince of a fellow
tucks her into bed.

> *Maybe we'll get together*
> *if your father dies first.*

Mornings, she returns to her room
identical to the make-believe one –
same carpet, lamps and clothes,
even the same seascape we gave Dad.

> *How can there be two of everything?*
> *How can I pay for both rooms?*

When I point out
that her stories don't stand up,
she giggles like a girl caught in her lies,

> *Ask your father. He goes there too.*

A Wealth of Extra Parts

A poet's is the most unpoetical of any existence because he has no identity – he is continually . . . filling some other body.

– John Keats

The Theatre

The Greeks named us *prosopa*
as if we did not exist beyond the masks
we wear, a hundred faces
we put on every day
of our tragi-comic lives
while the dancers dance
and the chorus sings on.

I stand between mirrors
amazed at endless images of
my self – the bridge
I am between past and future versions.
Yet the face behind the mask
does not change or age.

The physics of it is beyond me:
my clones clowning around –
Klondike girls on stage
doing the cancan in a sexy red chorus line.

In aerobics class we keep time to the music,
stretch for the ceiling, the ideal shape.
I check to make sure;
no one is more flexible than I.

My sisters and I are young women again
playing dress-up. We mince and prance
in see-through clothes and platform shoes.

I kid myself –
these brittle moments of eternity
will shatter when I leave the room.

Umbra Nihili

All human life sits under the shadow of nothingness.
                     — *Meister Eckhardt*

My body is a mirror image, a Rorschach
folded in half, a wealth of extra parts.
Arm arm ear ear eye eye,

I echo ovary ovary breast breast.
A Siamese twin
joined at heart and liver and spine.

But I never see my   self. The body
is always one step ahead.
I look over my shoulder,
                 the belly vanishes.

I assume a head but can't see
my face though I check the mirror
to prove I am here,
                 if only in reverse.

I can never be too sure,
straddling two voids as I do,
coming from nothing,
                 going nowhere.

The Ocean and Wilderness I Am

for Shendra

My niece dissected arms last month;
now she's doing legs. The class is working up
to a whole cadaver. She tells me
there's a tendon in the hand that splits
to let another pass through
like thread through a needle.
And two little bones
float under the foot
so we can stand on tiptoe.

I travel with her, explore
this *terra incognita* –
the ocean and wilderness I am.

The doctor shows me an X-ray of my leg,
a geography I need to learn.
Femur, tibia, fibula, patella
have carried my weight for sixty years.
They stack and fit together
like an Inca wall without mortar.
As if I have an expiry date,
the doctor points out
the patella has sprouted bony spurs
to cushion the blows as the knee slips
sideways, bone grinding bone.

Flustration

Rude blushes infuse
my breast, flow into
the roots of my hair,
flood belly and legs
like warm pee in a
dream that drips down
to the soles of my feet
and back up again.
I am flustered in my midst
by auroras that astonish
no one. My dyslexic body
is upside out, inside down.
The heart chakra
is out of whack.
I flush with the whoosh
of ravens' wings. I flash
like a Christmas tree
syncopated in red.
At an age when I ought
to be contemplating
the soul, my body
is a heat pump
with a thermostat
out of control.

A Certain Age

The woman grabs her dewlap,
It's this I hate. Pinches her jowls,
And these! She's considering
a facelift, an eyelid clip
for Christmas, a body make-over
to get rid of the bubble wrap.

Her dyed hair is full of dead ends.
The sheen is gone,
the multi-coloured strands of youth.
Every day she parades in the mirror,
Death jeers, *Here's looking at you.*

She will be her own anachronism –
a soul out of step with a body.
A face with a slick bony look
like one the undertaker creates –
the old Smoothie

transformed mother into a stranger
with high forehead, satin cheeks.
He wiped her battles clean away,
her flashing anger, her small joys.

A woman is more than a mannequin
dressing, re-dressing
as she descends the runway of years.
She is a piecework from heaven
that frays and fades.

The eternal seamstress grabs us all –
even gell-packed dolls with telling scars –
and she picks out every stitch
in her search for the priceless original.

Motorcycle Accident

A blow-out,
          and she is flung into space.

Time shrivels to details
recorded by some part of her
that watches. For once, her mind
does not chatter. There is nothing to do
caught on the cusp of here and now.
Surely, she dreams these blinding lights,
red wailing syncopated with shouts.
Clocks do not melt, nor people fly.
Surely, she is a bystander
to someone else's story, the friend
who said, *I want to come back as you.*
Yet how familiar the uprooting was,
the crumpled landing in the eye of the storm.

To Be

*Quién puede enseñarme a no ser,
a vivir sin seguir viviendo?*

— Estravagario, *Pablo Neruda*

The last tenant died of cancer
but the day I move in, there she is
dressed in gown and jewels.
I resist an impulse to shake hands,
make polite conversation.

Each night she waits for me
in the black and white tiled bathroom
that resembles a hospital ward.
Each night she trails me
past the locked cupboard where
her morphine is stored,
back to the master bedroom
where she died, where I sleep.

In my dreams she peers in mirrors
to convince herself she is gone
but *claroscuro* images
turn out to be me. Shadows
that lie on the floor
are mine and the moon's alone.

No one ever comes to collect
her effects stored in the garage.
There she leads me one day
to help myself
to a book by Neruda —
Estravagario –
someone who roams in bizarre ways.

Bad Girl

A stranger in the super market shouts at me,
You're a fucking Nazi middle-class bitch,
because I talk back when he orders me
to get my cart in line. So I do what he says.

Customers at the other tills avoid
my eyes. I duck my head, bite my tongue,
feel guilty for the asparagus I bought,
camembert and filet mignon.
He has bags of bulk food in his cart.

I make excuses for him: the job he lost,
the fight he had with his wife.
I am back in Grade Three, alone
in the cloakroom, waiting for the strap
because I talked out of turn.

I watch snow melt under forty small coats
in puddles on dark oiled floors.
I listen for a lull
in the classroom, the teacher's step.
One hand clutches air, the other is

outstretched. Afterwards, they feel
shapeless like woollen mittens
flung on the radiator to dry,
sizzling with a life of their own.

Gossip

OE *godsibb*, orig. *god-parent, related to God*

My golf partner has *never heard*
the likes of it. An eighty-year-old
divorced his wife of forty years
and married an alcoholic. Now *the old coot*
has left her for a thirty-year-old *bimbo.*
You'd think someone that age
would have more sense.

I don't want to listen to tittle tattle, clishma claver, gup and poop
But I do.
We girls feel safe when we stick together,
lick our suckers, swear not to tell.

On the way to the tee, we drive right by
a mockingbird in the acacia –
drab little busybody up before dawn
flicking her tail. Flibbertigibbet,
she sings every birdsong but her own.

The Corset-Maker

photos from Vogue *magazine*

The corset-maker haunts me: vapid black eyes,
skeletal forehead. I mistrust his studied repose.
Unruly black hairs curl on the back of his
hands – alive, defiant, sensual like
wayward pubic hair or the down
on a man's back – ancient
vestiges of fangs and
transformations.
I turn the page.
His eighteen-inch waist
is squeezed and scruzed into a
red satin corset he designed to wear
day and night. His hands – each
rebellious hair out of sight – thrust
casually in the pockets of his trousers
which hang belted below the hips in a
make-believe hourglass figure without

a head, and the head
I envision, hovering
around the bloodless body
like a soul near death, unsure
if it wants to cross over or
be stitched back on
by a sorcerer's
sleight-of-hand.

Stigmata

I have eighteen piercings;
I used to have twenty,
the young woman brags to her friends.
Six earrings in each ear – a rod
of curtain rings, an ear-splitting array.
A ring punctures the left eyebrow.
My eyes sweep her body,
pinpointing perforations,
speculating on the missing two.

Bound feet come to mind, chastity belts,
clitoridectomies – all the brutalities.
But this girl is her own property.
No biker with *I love father*
tattoed on her breast,
no adulteress labelled with shame.
She is blemished but unbranded,

delicate parts riddled and studded
with gold badges. A female Christ,
she sports stigmata with pride.
Follow me, she invites. *Come and*
run your tongue around my scars.

jenni+pooh.bear.com

*Without a camera, I probably
would have always been a nobody.*
          – *Jennifer Ringley*

stripped down to bare essentials
jenni clips her toenails   takes a bath
sits topless at the computer
has sex with a friend

she lives in front of cameras
as if they don't exist
a project in cyberspace
not an exhibitionist she says
just an ordinary girl
whose first love was
winnie the pooh

you can check her page
with a mouse and modem
a new vignette
every three minutes

with twenty million hits a day
she's her own paparraza
truly virtual   walking the edge
with peeping toms
she can't put her finger on

The Slave – Fantasy by an Unknown Artist

In the crowded market they arouse no interest,
four men in *burqas* doing business:
a young Venus – peach breasts, pubic fuzz.
She is tethered by a bearded African
who looms behind clutching her robe to his chest.
On the cobblestones, a limp dog lies belly-up.

The Arab buyer weighs her merits. Is she docile?
Will she breed? Does she bear scars?
He disguises his eagerness. For a virgin
the asking price is high.

Only his eyes and nose are visible
and a large hand that pries apart
the girl's lips as if she were horseflesh
though she does not shudder
as a horse would with rippling withers.
Her hip thrusts out. Her look is artless,
inviting him to fondle the nipples, to slide
his long fingers slowly, slowly down her thighs
to the soft mound, to waken her
while all the men are watching.

The New Messiah

*In Britain, 300 women have taken out insurance
against having a virgin birth by act of God in
expectation of a second coming in the year 2000.*
                    – The Globe and Mail

She has no desire
to be blessed among women,
raped by a godhead,
no matter how soulful his looks.

She is fearful of favours,
avoids clairvoyants and learned men,
suspects the synergy of moonlight.
Portents are everywhere.
Sun's rays kiss her nape,
clouds overshadow her.
Sly breezes lift her skirts,
breathe along her thighs.
A woodpecker raps on the fir
and she hears creation
in the letters of her name.
Pebbles arrange themselves
in patterns of doom.

When night stalks the streets
she double-locks the doors
before climbing into bed.
Her dreams shimmer
with small blue souls.

L'Acte Gratuit

After shoving a young woman
into the path of a subway train,
he showed no remorse,
mumbled something
about losing his job.
Or was it his home?
A voice told him, *She's
the type who laughs at you.*
Perhaps he objected to her
walking in front of him,
ghosted a woman he loathed,
a look of disdain. Perhaps
he was overcome
by the rush of stale air.
Stampeding wheels
derailed his mind.
Perhaps he wanted to play
God, feel omnipotent.
Perhaps none of this is true.
He just had the urge to push,
the way he has the urge to piss.
He could have so easily
not done it. Afterwards,
he had a smoke
while he waited for the police.
Perhaps he was thinking:
women get what they ask for.
Perhaps he was thinking
nothing at all.

Forgive us Our Trespasses

In Anza Borrego desert, we pull off the road
for a breath of silence. At the lookout
an untidy hand-lettered sign: **Peace and Love**.
A tall man waits, Ghandi-like
with knobby knees, slack skin.
No saint wandering in the wilderness
but latter-day prophet
in red shorts and yellow T-shirt.

He preaches love, hands us a Xerox
from Dear Abby, "Fasting from Resentment".

And a quotation from Matthew:
"For iF ye Forgive Men Their Treaspasses (sic),
your Heavenly Father will also Forgive you."
The writing is child-like, the "f's"
capitalized, like pitchforks.

He approaches as we stand looking over
a chasm called the Font –
ancient hills baptized in fire and brimstone.
Too bad we're not like her,
he points at the dog I whistle back from the edge.
Now, she doesn't give you Hell
when you come home late, does she?

On a Bus to the Everglades

I picture the straddling mangroves,
alligators in armoured sleep,
pink clouds of flamingos.

The bus driver – grizzled curls,
singsong Caribbean voice –
manoeuvres the wheel, his arm a cog
in a well-oiled machine, an arm
sculpted from mahogany,
each vein, artery, tendon
articulate strings under the skin.

From my seat, the arm seems disconnected,
the lost arm of a Greek statue
retrieved from the sea.

Suddenly, I feel guilty for reducing him,
the way men have reduced women
since the days of Pompeii
to genitalia scribbled on walls.

But I am not a woman who collects
body parts. The grace of the man –
his rhythm, his timing –
this is the way I used to dance,
a song strumming my body –
this is the way I used to make love.

                And the Everglades?

In a jet boat, we roar and sluice
across the saw grass swamp,
scattering every bird. I see
one old alligator with a sore on his back
who waits in the same spot every day
for the boatboys to throw him some bread.

Alfred Hitchcock Dolls

Baby Boomers are reaching back to nostalgic themes, says the chairman of Madame Alexander Dolls, *and Alfred Hitchcock generates quite a buzz.*
                     — *The Desert Sun, Feb.,1998*

The Birds Doll
comes with birds attached to her hands and feet,
tangled in her hair and fur coat.
A smiling saint of Assisi, she waits
to be martyred by beaks and wings.

The Psycho Doll
is towel-clad, standing in a bathtub
stamped **PSYCHO** in broken letters.
On the shower curtain, a silhouette
is about to slash her throat
yet no terror shows on her face.
She has no vulva either —
essential parts are left out
to protect the children.

A little girl is no fool.
She'll pluck the birds from the doll's hair.
She'll rip away the curtain-killer,
bury him deep under toys in her chest.
Clutching a toy gun under the covers
she'll take the doll to bed
and talk her into being brave.

Touchstones

for Ron

1

After the fight, I went to Vancouver,
considered a new life floating in a fishbowl,
caged in cement and solitary steel,
geraniums in pots on the balcony,
traffic jungles in the streets. Below,
a bushy beard argues with himself
rushing by. A goitred woman,
painted white – ancient geisha –
slides along graffiti façades.

2

I could have chosen this, quit
our rainbow garden, cedar house by the sea.
Anchors I know. Here,
we came in summer with our children
when dreams were intact. Randall
went scuba-diving, speared a ling cod
whose green flesh I threw away
thinking it was spoiled.
Andrea built driftwood houses.
In autumn we went back
overseas
to gather the mosaic of our lives.

These gifts I cherish, and you.
For without witness, I, too,
am white powdered face
and shouts in the streets.

Andrea de Los Angeles

for my daughter

1

Your mother leaves your sister   then you
She drops you off in the Santiago slums
at Senora Pastora's   the woman named
shepherdess who looks after children

So what can the good woman do
but keep you   Little mother
you earn your way
burping babies   changing diapers

learn to suck a lemon-peel clean
chew a chicken-bone till it disappears

2

The first visit we take you with our son
to the foothills of the Andes
to pick flowers   collect insects
You're in a swirling field of daisies

a small seven-year-old   with a burden
of long chestnut hair   chubby body
squeezed into a blue sweater
a hand-me-down from the Home

We speak Spanish with foreign accents
outlandish English
You don't say a word in any tongue
just stand with lampblack eyes
watching and weighing
us

pulling us into your orbit
like three moons dancing
attendance on you
fantasizing a family of four

3

Back home   wanting to know you
I bring out crayons   You draw
an egg-yolk sun   colour
a world outlined in black
grinning trees with hands on their hips
birds with crooked smiles

A black figure with long hair floats
in the corner of the page   huge arms
outspread towards a magenta house
whose windows and doors
shine like jewels

4

The second visit
you take some apples from the kitchen
stuff them in your pockets   in case
you aren't invited back

We walk through
a wealth of warm rooms   offer you
a bedroom of your own

We ask if you want to come live with us
Si   you reply without a pause   *Si*
as if you always knew you would
alight on us